O Taste and See That the Lord Is Good

Enriching Your Teaching Ministry

Abingdon Press

Nashville

Abingdon Press
O TASTE AND SEE
THAT THE LORD IS GOOD

ISBN: 0-687-026067

Unless otherwise noted, Scripture quotations are from the New Revised Standard Version of the Bible. Copyright ©1989 by the Division of Christian Education of the National Council of Churches of Christ in the USA. Used by permission.

Editor: LeeDell Stickler
Production Editor: Kerry Blackwood
Production and Design Manager:
R.E. Osborne
Designer: Vicki Williamson
Illustrator: Megan Jeffery

02 03 04 05 06 07 08 09 10 11– 10 9 8 7 6 5 4 3 2 1

MANUFACTURED IN
THE UNITED STATES OF AMERICA

O TASTE AND SEE THAT THE LORD IS GOOD

Contents

O Taste and See That the Lord Is Good

A Letter to Teachers

Section 4

Planning the Worship

O TASTE AND SEE THAT THE LORD IS GOOD

STARTING WITH THE BRAIN

O TASTE AND SEE THAT THE LORD IS GOOD

Exercise 1:

Sing, Move, Praise God

The more we learn about the brain, the more we discover the importance of music. In fact, not only is the brain designed for music and rhythm, but music has a positive, measurable, and lasting educational benefit. Music is not just a "right brained" activity. In fact, it is recognized that listening to music engages the entire brain. Music in the Sunday school not only acts as an enrichment, but it also does three other things:

- Music can act as a stimulator and perk up the children, or it can act as a calming agent, helping the children to relax. Music directly affects the state of the learner and the state of the learner also affects the learning.
- Music acts as a carrier. Melody of the music is the vehicle for the words. Boys and girls quickly pick up the words to new songs because it is the melody that helps them learn the new songs. (How many of us turn to the "Alphabet Song" whenever we have to alphabetize anything?)
- Music primes the neural pathways. The brain is constantly working. What makes this more efficient is the speed, sequence, and strength of the connections the brain engages. Music can help with this. Think of the times when you have put on music to help you with a routine task, such as cleaning house or driving.

Music plays a significant role in enhancing learning skills. Music is a language unto itself and can enhance the abilities of children who don't excel in other learning styles. As teachers we have always understood the distinct appeal of music to the children. Now researchers are discovering that music is not only an enrichment, it is a particularly effective teaching tool. It builds creativity, concentration, coordination, and self-discipline.

Jump, Turn, Praise!

Gonna jump down, turn around
(*Jump; turn around*)
clap my hands and praise God,
(*Clap hands; raise arms*)
Gonna jump down, turn around
(*Jump; turn around*)
clap my hands and praise!
(*Clap hands; raise arms*)

Gonna jump down, turn around
(*Jump; turn around*)
stomp my feet and praise God,
(*Stomp feet; raise arms*)
Gonna jump down, turn around
(*Jump; turn around*)
stomp my feet and praise!
(*Stomp feet; raise arms*)

Gonna jump down, turn around
(*Jump; turn around*)
pat my head and praise God,
(*Pat head; raise arms*)
Gonna jump down, turn around
(*Jump; turn around*)
pat my head and praise!
(*Pat head; raise arms*)

Gonna jump down, turn around
(*Jump; turn around*)
swing my hips and praise God,
(*Swing hips; raise arms*)
Gonna jump down, turn around
(*Jump; turn around*)
swing my hips and praise!
(*Swing hips; raise arms*)

Gonna jump down, turn around
(*Jump; turn around*)
shake myself and praise God,
(*Wiggle whole body; raise arms*)
Gonna jump down, turn around
(*Jump; turn around*)
shake myself and praise!
(*Wiggle whole body; raise arms*)

WORDS: Daphna Flegal

O TASTE AND SEE THAT THE LORD IS GOOD

Test Your Brain Knowledge

Beside each statement write "T" if you believe the statement to be true and "F" if you believe the statement to be false. Write "U" if you are undecided.

_____1. The human brain weighs less than 2 pounds.

_____2. During your lifetime you will use about 10 percent of your brain's capacity.

_____3. The human brain has about 100 billion brain cells at birth.

_____4. The brain prefers words over rhyme, music, and pattern.

_____5. The brain can only pay attention to one thing at a time.

_____6. The human brain thinks in color.

_____7. The brain is like a sponge.

_____8. The brain learns best between ten and sixteen years of age.

_____9. The brain is never NOT paying attention.

_____10. Humor is an excellent way to enhance learning.

_____11. What you eat really does affect your brain.

_____12. Your brain requires at least four to five glasses of water per day.

_____13. The brain has difficulty comprehending very large numbers.

_____14. Infants learn new words at the rate of about 50 words per week.

_____15. The only way to get information into the brain is through our senses.

_____16. When the emotional content of learning is too high, the brain shifts into overdrive and becomes more efficient.

_____17. Practice is not an important part of learning.

_____18. During the learning process, the brain requires no downtime to process information.

Answers

1. **False.** The human brain weighs less than two pounds.
(*The brain actually weighs about three pounds and is the size of a cabbage.*)

2. **False** During your lifetime you will use about ten percent of your brain's capacity. (*You will likely only use about 2 to 3% of your brain's capacity.*)

3. **True** The human brain has about 100 billion brain cells at birth.

4. **False** The brain prefers words over rhyme, music, and pattern.
(*The brain prefers rhyme, rhythm, and pattern over words.*)

5. **True** The brain can only pay attention to one thing at a time.

6. **True** The human brain thinks in color.

7. **False** The brain is like a sponge.

8. **False** The brain learns best between ten and sixteen years of age.
(*The brain learns best between birth and ten years.*)

9. **True** The brain is never NOT paying attention.

10. **True** Humor is an excellent way to enhance learning.

11. **True** What you eat really does affect your brain.

12. **True** Your brain requires at least four to five glasses of water per day.

13. **True** The brain has difficulty comprehending very large numbers.

14. **True** Infants learn new words at the rate of about 50 words per week.

15. **True** The only way to get information into the brain is through our senses.

16. **False** When the emotional content of learning is too high, the brain shifts into overdrive and becomes more efficient. (*Just the opposite is true. The brain shuts down and becomes less efficient.*)

17. **False** Practice is not an important part of learning. (*Not only does practice make perfect, it also makes permanent.*)

18. **False** During the learning process, the brain requires no downtime to process information. (*The brain needs time to process and reflect on all new bits of information in order for it to make meaning.*)

O TASTE AND SEE THAT THE LORD IS GOOD

This Is Your Brain

- The human brain weighs about 3 pounds fully developed. Think of a large head of cabbage.
- The brain consists of 100 billion brain cells or neurons at birth. This is compared to a mouse which has 5 million and a monkey that has 10 billion. Researchers estimate only about 1/10 of one percent of them will be used.
- A human being uses only about 2-3% of the total brain's capacity.
- The brain doesn't like words. The brain does like rhythm, rhyme, and pattern.
- The brain thinks in color.
- The brain is energy inefficient. It is about 2% of the body weight and yet it uses 20% of the body's energy.
- The brain learns best between birth and ten years.
- The brain is never NOT paying attention.
- The brain is mostly water.
- The brain really is affected by what you eat. Brain foods are: green leafy vegetables, salmon, nuts, lean meat, fresh fruits, yogurt and milk.

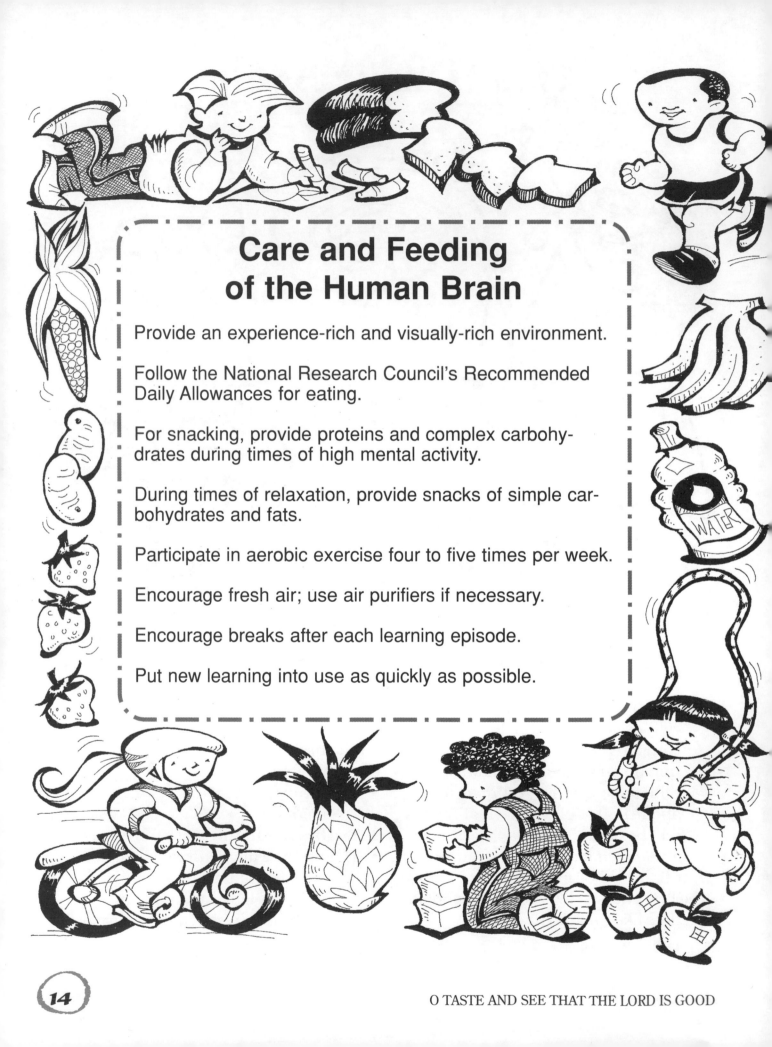

Care and Feeding of the Human Brain

Provide an experience-rich and visually-rich environment.

Follow the National Research Council's Recommended Daily Allowances for eating.

For snacking, provide proteins and complex carbohydrates during times of high mental activity.

During times of relaxation, provide snacks of simple carbohydrates and fats.

Participate in aerobic exercise four to five times per week.

Encourage fresh air; use air purifiers if necessary.

Encourage breaks after each learning episode.

Put new learning into use as quickly as possible.

O TASTE AND SEE THAT THE LORD IS GOOD

What's the Buzz?

by Barbara Bruce

We have learned more about the brain in the last three decades than in all of human history combined. Researchers can actually see the brain functioning on CAT scans, PET scans, and functional MRIs. They can track the process of thinking. These techniques may provide the keys to unlocking the secrets of learning disabilities and provide better ways to reach all children.

The brain is the most amazing organism known to humankind. It is divided into two hemispheres, left controlling the right side of the body and right controlling the left side of the body. The hemispheres are connected by fibrous tissue called the Corpus Callosum, which allows information to pass from one hemisphere to the other. Historically the left hemisphere deals more with concrete issues—words, numbers, order, and sequence. The right hemisphere deals with pictures, music, and creativity. For learning to be complete, you **must** engage both hemispheres of the brain. This means you read words and look at pictures; you ask logical questions and silly questions that encourage both critical and creative thinking; you encourage using both hands in doing activities for bilateral connections; you put something in logical order and then discover another way to look at it.

The brain must have an environment that is safe to function at its best. If your child feels stress from the threat of sarcasm, ridicule, or humiliation, the brain shuts down learning.

The brain has a quality known as "plasticity" that allows it to develop to meet the unique needs of each person. No two brains develop in exactly the same way. You have the power and ability to mold your child's brain by the experiences you provide. Studies show that children raised in an enriched environment strengthen brain connections. This means you go to museums, listen to music, take trips, and provide books and other learning resources.

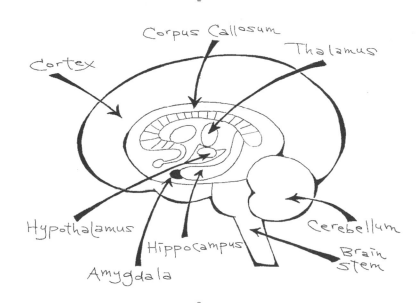

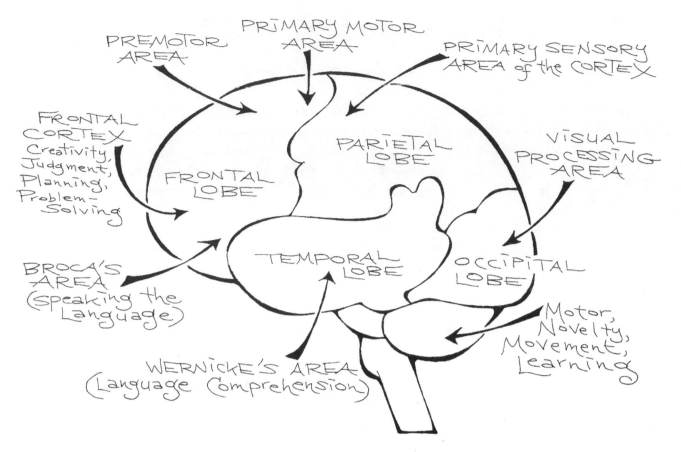

The brain must be kept active for optimum health. Just as with your physical muscles, your brain "muscles" must be kept fit. This means you talk with (not down to) your children, ask and answer questions, read together, do puzzles (both word and picture), and encourage problem-solving in age-appropriate ways. Focus on active learning in which your children are fully involved.

The brain requires water, oxygen, and good nutrition to function at peak levels. This means you encourage children to drink water, not soft drinks; you encourage movement—running and playing games that require large muscle development and force blood circulation—rather than sitting for hours in front of the TV; you provide healthy meals and snacks loaded with fruits and vegetables.

As a teacher, you may only come in contact with these children for one hour a week. But still you can play a part in directing the development of each child's brain. You want the children to remember the life lessons they encounter at church. You want them to learn the Bible stories. You want them to form a lasting relationship with Jesus Christ. There is no reason you cannot use the best teaching techniques possible. Remember to stimulate both brain hemispheres, minimize stress, enrich your environment, encourage physical and mental activity, and provide good nutrition.

Adapted from *Exploring Faith With Families, Fall 2002,* © 2002 Cokesbury.

O TASTE AND SEE THAT THE LORD IS GOOD

The Role of Stress

By Barbara Bruce

For decades there has been the discussion of which is more important to human development—nature (what you are born with) or nurture (the environment). Scientists still disagree. But many, including Marian Diamond at The University of California at Berkeley, believe that nurture plays an enormous role in brain formation. The brain reacts to the formation of chemicals. There are various types of chemicals produced according to the environment in which brain growth occurs.

The first and most important consideration is to eliminate stress. When children feel threatened, either physically or psychologically, they revert to a basic functioning mode of self-preservation. Since there is no separation between mind and body, the brain behaves in the same way. Learning becomes less important than self-care.

As a teacher, you have no control over the physical and psychological climate in the children's homes. But you do have control over the class environment when the children are with you. As an effective teacher, you must do all in your power to eliminate threats (real or imagined) including sarcastic remarks, ridicule, or berating—any form of humiliation. The stress that these experiences cause triggers the release of a chemical called cortisol. Prolonged exposure to this chemical may cause the death of brain cells, which leads to long-term difficulties including depression and inability to think logically. High cortisol levels make children more susceptible to many diseases.

Watch for signs of high stress in your arena. Make the changes necessary to

remove the causes of high stress. Stress is the most common cause of poor performance in otherwise healthy children. As important as it is to deter physical threats, psychological threats form scars that may never disappear. Think about your own history. Can you recall a time when you were ridiculed or put down? How long ago was that? How did it feel? The brain remembers.

Threats imposed in the class (like "If you don't stop that right now, I'll ...") cause damage to self-esteem and morale.* Some may seem innocuous, but they still damage a child's sense of self. The brain remembers.

As a teacher, you can establish good thinking habits as you and the children set reasonable boundaries for behavior. You can explain and model cause and effect. Both of these activities promote brain-strengthening skills and avoid brain-harming threats and stress.

While eliminating stress is crucial to the children's well-being, creating a positive environment for the children to learn and grow is also extremely important. An environment that focuses on success and good feelings helps the brain to produce chemicals called endorphins that help a child to relax and feel good. Therefore, it is imperative for you to praise your children as often as possible.

The brain becomes flooded with positive chemistry and flourishes when a child is praised. Phrases such as "Good job," "Nice work," and "I'm so proud of you," cannot be said too often. We know it takes a four-to-one praise-to-criticism ratio to keep children on track. Find ways to praise the children in your class. First eliminate threats, then add praise as much as possible.

*Editor's Note: A threat is not the same as explaining a logical consequence. (For example: "If you don't stop that right now, you might hurt somebody, and I know you don't really want to hurt anybody.")

Adapted from *Exploring Faith With Families, Winter 2002-03*, © 2002 Cokesbury.

Barbara Bruce is a longtime educator with a passion for helping people learn to their greatest potential. She is an author and trainer in Multiple Intelligences and Brain Research. Her books and seminars focus on the amazing brain and how it learns. Barbara serves the Rush United Methodist Church near Rochester, NY.

O TASTE AND SEE THAT THE LORD IS GOOD

Putting Your Brain in Gear

1. Your Nose Knows

The smell organs are connected directly to the higher cognitive centers of the brain. The sensors in our nose and our brain allow us to recognize ten thousand different smells. There are seven categories of smells: minty, floral, ethereal (for example, a pear), musky, resinous (for example, camphor), putrid (for example, rotten eggs), and pungent (for example, vinegar).

On the table in front of you are five numbered jars. In each jar is a different smell. Open the lids carefully and sniff the inside. What is the first thing that the smell brings to mind? Write that on the line.

Jar #1: _____

Jar #2: _____

Jar #3: _____

Jar #4: _____

Jar #5: _____

Did you know?

- Not all people are sensitive to the same smells and sensitivities can be extremely disruptive.
- Smells tend to affect productivity: peppermint improves performance, lavender increases alertness.
- The smell of green apples tends to make a room feel larger.
- The smell of vanilla is relaxing and induces sleep.
- The smell of baking cookies or breads increases helping behavior.

2. Time Warp

In the center of your table there is a small ball. Form a circle with your group. Let one of the group members be the time keeper and step out of the group. The rest of the group will begin to pass the ball to one another. Everyone in the group must touch the ball and the touching must be in the same order. The idea is to follow the same pattern and do it as quickly as possible. The time keeper will "time" each round. Continue to ask the group, "Can you do this any quicker?"

After several tries, someone should get the idea that lining up in order and passing the ball is a more efficient way to pass the ball. The group probably made the assumption that they had to stay in a circle.

Theory: The brain loves patterns and sometimes needs to be forced to look at things in a different way.

3. Take a Brain Break

When you feel the need for an energy break, stand up. Then either in the air or on paper with a marker in each hand, draw the same configuration with both hands (for example, a figure eight). Keep this up for sixty seconds.

Theory: The arm movements increase the blood flow and oxygen to the brain. The dual movements activate both sides of the brain.

O TASTE AND SEE THAT THE LORD IS GOOD

4. Chunking

Our working memory is the place where information is processed. Working memory can handle only a few "chunks" of information at one time. The first hook for semantic memory is meaning. The second hook is patterns created by prior knowledge or experience. Of the two, meaning is the most important.

Here is a string of letters. Spend the next one minute trying to learn the sequence. Then close the book and write down the sequence as you remember it on a sheet of paper. How much did you get correct? The letters have been grouped together to make it easier.

AM APH DUS AFB ICI AFD RJF KTN T

Theory: The brain thrives on meaning, not random information.

Note: Rewrite the letters in the space here, but shift the space to the right by one. The patterns should be easier to remember then.

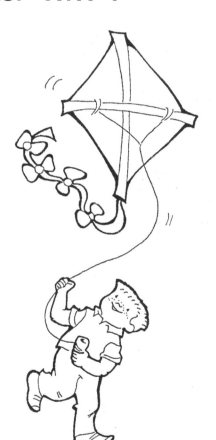

Exercise 4:

What's Your Image?

How do you see yourself as a teacher? Are you the super teacher, with everything under control? Are you the juggler, struggling to keep everything going? Are you the upstream paddler, working hard but never getting anywhere? Look in the mirror here. Draw the image of how you see yourself as a teacher.

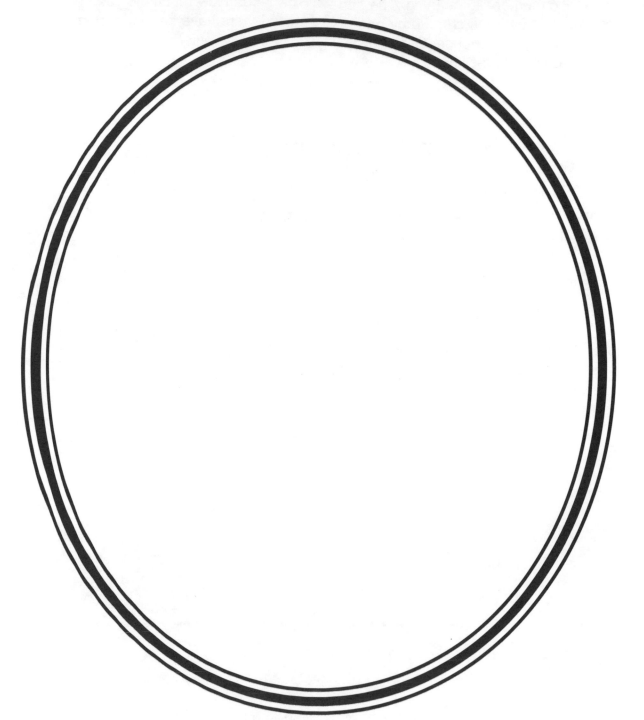

O TASTE AND SEE THAT THE LORD IS GOOD

The Ways We Learn

24

How Do Children Learn?

by LeeDell Stickler

What the human brain does best is to learn. When the human brain learns, the brain rewires itself. New connections are made between the neurons. Each new experience, each new encounter, each new behavior is incorporated into the brain.

Scientists are not really sure how this learning takes place, but they know it happens because they can measure it. As teachers, we are concerned with learning. The efforts into lesson planning and pre-class preparation are all directed toward the goal of learning—whether it is a Bible verse we want the children to recall or a Bible story.

So what is learning? Perhaps if we understand this, then we will better be able to be effective teachers.

- **We are either doing something we already know how to do or we are doing something new.**

When a child is learning something new, the brain is actively at work, but it is more inefficient than if the child were simply expanding on knowledge that is already there. Repetition creates more efficient pathways in the brain, but new knowledge stimulates new areas of the brain. Less of the brain is used as a task is learned.

- **Learning and memory are two sides of a coin.**

The only evidence of learning is memory. But we are all aware of how frustrating this can be. Scientists are still unsure exactly how this happen. They are, however, absolutely sure, that lasting learning is essential to the actual process of learning.

- **Learning and behavior, while related, are not the same thing.**

A child may learn something, but this learning may or may not change his or her behavior. Behavior can be affected by a child's emotional status, which as we know, is affected by many other stimuli. Emotions can also be affected by memories. Learning and retaining learning is much more complex than anything we can imagine.

- **The end result of learning is intelligence.**

Intelligence is not governed by the size of the brain. A dolphin has a *bigger* brain. A rat's brain has *more* cell density than a human brain. So those are not the only factors. The key to getting smarter is for the brain to develop more connections between the brain cells and not losing the already existing connections. These connections are what help children "figure things out."

If learning is our inevitable goal, then we ought to value the process of learning as much as the results. A healthy and growing brain needs more than a narrow view of what learning really is. A brain needs to be challenged, not by always seeking the "right" answer, but the encouragements of exploration, of alternative thinking, and of creative insights. As teachers, it is our job to create the environment that fosters learning.

Activity based learning is the most productive form of learning. When children get involved with their whole bodies, then learning is more likely to take place.

O TASTE AND SEE THAT THE LORD IS GOOD

Ten Ways to Create a Brain-Friendly Classroom

by Barbara Bruce

This is a very exciting and fascinating time for brain research as it relates to learning. As educators, this technology can be used in your Sunday school. The brain is created to make meaning. You can help by creating a brain-friendly environment. Include these simple tasks and watch as your children become more interested and excited about learning. Test the ideas in your classroom. Include the children in your experiment. Tell them you are trying out some new ideas to help make their brains function better. Ask for their input.

1. The brain functions best in a safe environment.

Establish rules with your class. When children have a part in creating the rules, they react well to enforcing them.

Do not allow ridicule or mocking. Children must have respect for themselves and each other. All ideas are accepted, not necessarily agreed with, just accepted with an open and questioning mind.

Insist on cooperation. Teach children how to work together and appreciate each other's gifts and talents.

State consequences with children accepting the responsibility of their actions.

Create an environment of trust. Children trust you to behave in certain ways. Misbehavior is not allowed; fairness is the rule; mistreatment of another is called into account; and everyone is treated in ways that show appreciation for all God's children

Use child-size furniture. Call children by name. Children function best when they feel welcomed.

2. The brain functions best when emotions are engaged.

Emotions are powerful learning tools. When you tell children a Bible story, it can be simply an interesting story, or it can help children to understand that

truths of the Bible live today. Engage children's emotions in the story. For example, in the story of Joseph and his colorful coat, ask questions such as, "Have you ever been jealous of a brother/sister? Have you ever felt your parent(s) liked you or one of your siblings better?" Engaging the emotional content of the story helps the brain kick into high gear, and the story becomes imprinted through the powerful handle of emotions. A story about someone long ago now becomes your story because you know how it feels to be jealous, and you understand Joseph's brothers' anger with him.

Stop throughout the story and ask how they think that character is feeling or what they might do in a similar situation.

3. The brain functions best when there is an enriched environment.

In scientific studies, animals performed better in an environment that was full of color and interesting items upon which to focus. Translating this research means your Sunday school classroom is brain-friendly when it is rich with interest. The content you are studying needs to be represented in the room.

Use maps, pictures, and artifacts to draw attention and engage the brain in more ways than words alone. Items that focus children's attention or hook them into the lesson will give you incredible rewards of concentration.

4. The brain functions best when you move.

Take "brain breaks" by having the children stand up and move. This activity can be incorporated into the lesson in enriching ways. Ask the children to move as if they were showing off the new coat Dad got for them, or as if they were the brothers bowing down to Joseph; or take a long, slow walk around the outskirts of the room as if they were walking with a caravan to Egypt.

5. The brain functions best when you connect to past experience.

When you make connections to what is already known, the brain has the ability to hook onto previous knowledge. Seldom do you teach in a vacuum. Children know something about the content you are teaching.

Ask them to tell you what they know, then hook the new information onto what they already know. In the case of Joseph, the children know about jealousy, anger, favoritism, feeling left out, and forgiveness.

6. The brain functions best when you focus on specifics.

Encourage children to look for specific information. If you are watching a video on Joseph, ask the children to note the content of the dreams that Joseph had concerning his brothers, or the dreams that Pharaoh had. At the end of the video, ask the children to describe the dreams Joseph had. Ask, "Does this

O TASTE AND SEE THAT THE LORD IS GOOD

explanation help you to understand why the brothers were so upset with Joseph?" Or ask them to describe the dreams that Pharaoh had. Ask, "How did Joseph's interpreting (through God) of these dreams help him?" When children focus on specifics, their brains become more tuned in to the content.

When reading a story, ask the children to look for three specific points in the story and how these points help the story make sense. The more specific the question, the harder the brain works to learn.

When asking children to write something, have them describe in as much detail as they can. If they are writing a story about Joseph's brothers throwing him into the pit, ask them to describe the pit—how did it look, feel, smell? Have them put themselves in Joseph's place and describe his feelings.

7. The brain functions best when you reinforce learning in several ways.
The more ways the brain learns something, the more of an imprint the learning makes. This concept of Multiple Intelligences connects the "why" and the "how" of brain research to complete the picture. The newest wave of Sunday school interest is the Rotational Learning or The United Methodist

Publishing House's PowerXpress™. You can read more about this model from a variety of sources available.

Ask the children to close their eyes and tell you what they see, hear, and smell. Using a sensory approach helps the brain to connect the story, and incorporating the senses helps make brain connections. Think of the connections your brain makes to a special smell—baking bread or a garden in the hot sun. Our other senses work as well to connect meaning to our brains. When teaching about Joseph, you might include a "touch box" containing sheepskin, sand, a soft coat fabric, grain, and any other tactile items that will help to tell the story in a sensory way.

8. The brain functions best when you change pace.

Change the pace of learning occasionally to stimulate the brain. This does not mean you must change content, simply stand up and move, sing, stretch, or ask the children to talk to the person next to them about the story.

Use contrast. If you are doing a quiet activity, change to a song with the same content. If you are dancing, switch to a "close your eyes and think about" activity. The greater the contrast, the greater the stimulus to the brain.

O TASTE AND SEE THAT THE LORD IS GOOD

9. **The brain functions best when you take time to reflect and process information.**

Sustained focus in one intelligence sets the brain into "coast mode." Often children confined to sitting in one place while reading or following a pattern start to exhibit unwanted behavior or claim that they are bored. This occurs because the brain is programmed to incorporate a certain amount of information, then it must process that information before it can absorb anything else. Experts believe you can teach about seven bits of information and then you must stop and take time to incorporate that learning. The new information needs time to hook on to what is already at work in the brain.

Reflect on what has been learned at the end of every lesson. Begin the next lesson by reflecting on last week's lesson. This reflection is absolutely necessary for the brain to imprint new information.

More is not always better. The brain will respond by learning smaller bits of information that hook on to one another than to information overload. Too much information, which has not been processed, leads to frustration and brain shutdown.

10. **The brain functions best when it is used.**

Just as your body functions best when you exercise and strengthen muscles, your brain works best when it is used efficiently. Use your brain. Help it to work at optimum levels. It is easier than you think and will provide great rewards in enhancing children's learning and faith growth.

Adapted from *Children's Teacher, Vol. 9, No. 2, Winter 2001–02*, © 2001 Cokesbury.

Choosing Learning Activities

1. A learning activity should have purpose. It should enrich the experiences of the unit of study and help to fulfill the aims and purposes of the lesson.

2. A learning activity should be planned with the needs, interests, and capacities of the children in mind.

3. A learning activity should include work with the hands, work with the feet (carrying out some service project), work with the mind in creating stories, songs, litanies, and prayers.

4. A learning activity should lead to rich worship experiences where the children become aware of God and feel God's nearness.

5. A learning activity should be tried out by the teacher ahead of time so that she/he may be able to guide the children in carrying through a definite plan.

6. A learning activity should help the child discover deeper religious meanings and larger social relationships.

7. A learning activity should teach appreciation of others and give practice in cooperative living.

8. A learning activity should develop creative ability and help the child assume and carry out responsibilities.

9. A learning activity works best when both the children and the teacher participate in planning and working it out.

10. A learning activity is not just busywork. It is never something to just fill in time.

11. A learning activity should be planned to work toward specific goals in helping the children grow in Christian ways of thinking.

O TASTE AND SEE THAT THE LORD IS GOOD

Using the Multiple Intelligences

by Barbara Bruce

By increasing the use of all intelligences, you can approach the same topic from several different brain locations. This multiple stimulation creates many neural connections which increase the avenues your child has for recall and connection. Gardner et al. from Harvard University have been promoting the theory of Multiple Intelligences for over two decades. It fits so well with brain research, that it is difficult to separate the two.

The following are specific suggestions of ways to include the learning styles in your teaching:

Verbal/Linguistic (word smart)

Encourage talking and listening. Introduce new words each week and help the children learn them. Use them several times during the class. Make up poems. Tell the Bible stories rather than read them aloud. Encourage the children to react to the stories. Learn words in a different language. Bring in other resources that tell about the topic you are studying. Invite the children to talk about related events and circumstances.

Logical/Mathematical (number smart)

This learning style goes beyond math skills. It includes problem-solving, sequencing, and critical thinking skills. Invite the children to compare and contrast. Place things in logical order then illogical order. Practice valuing by rating things on a scale of 1-10. List foods, people, stories, objects, or needs by categories.

Visual/Spatial (picture smart)

Look at pictures as well as maps, graphs, videos. Help the children to get a sense of where they are in relation to other things—in your town or in the world. Draw, paint sculpt, carve in sand or snow. Bring in commercial books with pictures from the Holy Land or ancient cultures.

Musical/Rhythmic (music smart)

Don't forget the music. Invite the children to sing, tap out rhythms as they listen to the songs on the CD or cassette. Let the children write new words to a familiar tune, such as "Twinkle, Twinkle, Little Star." Let the children write or create music for a biblical passage. Listen to a variety of music and find things to appreciate about it. Connect classical music to Bible stories where possible. For example Handel's "Messiah" is great to use at both Christmas and Easter.

Body/Kinesthetic (body smart)

Engage the children's bodies in the teaching. Form postures to express concepts, move the way words sound, manipulate objects, build things with blocks or LEGOs, clay, or stones. Compare taste, touch, and smell items. Involve the children in physical games.

O TASTE AND SEE THAT THE LORD IS GOOD

Intrapersonal (self smart)

Practice the power of reflective thinking, journaling, quiet time, and thinking time. Model and encourage reflection—it is a powerful means of imprinting information on the brain. Provide a quiet time of personal prayer. Give children time to debrief knowledge before having to put it to work. Have the children compare their own feelings to the feelings of a Bible story character. Invite the children to travel to biblical locations in their minds.

Interpersonal (people smart)

Encourage the children to interact with one another. Put them together in small groups and give them projects to do as a team. Help them learn to read the reactions of others. Let them be in charge of planning a special snack, worship time, or celebration for the rest of the group. Each of these intelligences can be traced to a specific area of the brain. It makes sense then to strengthen and enrich many areas of the brain to stimulate and use all intelligences. Each time you strengthen brain cell connections, you provide a greater ability to recall information. Learning is easier when the connections have already been formed.

Exercise 5:

You've Got Style!

Each child in your class is unique. Each one has his or her own unique combination of gender, skin color, size, personality, and interests. But perhaps less obvious is the variety of unique ways the students in your class use to learn.

What is a learning style?

A learning style is the way a person perceives and processes information through his or her brain so that it becomes meaningful. Every person has a preferred learning style. It is not preferred because the person has chosen it; it is preferred because of the developmental factors that have made that way of learning the most effective for that particular person.

A person can have more than one learning style that helps them learn most effectively. But all persons can learn in many ways. They learn best, in fact, when they experience many different learning styles. The learning styles are all interconnected.

How do I recognize these learning styles?

Read through the descriptions of each of the following learning styles. Check off activities that you particularly like to do. Then go back and see where you have the most checkmarks. That will probably be your preferred learning style. Then think about the children in your class. You should be able to identify their learning styles simply by working with them.

How do I use learning styles to make teaching more effective?

Think variety! Provide activities in the class that use many different styles of learning. Recognize the fact that each of the boys and girls you teach may have a different learning style. This doesn't mean you have to use every learning style every Sunday. But in the course of teaching, try to select activities that reflect all the learning styles over a month or several weeks.

Recognize also that you have a preferred learning style too and it may not be one that you share with your children. Your job is to structure learning experiences that will enable others to learn. Experiment with new ways to teach just as you want your students to experiment with new ways to learn.

O TASTE AND SEE THAT THE LORD IS GOOD

Verbal Linguistic

In a nutshell: This learner loves words and language, both written and spoken.

Learns best by: This learner learns best by saying things aloud, hearing words spoken, and seeing words in print.

Activities:

- ❏ read, write, tell stories
- ❏ memorize names, dates, and trivia
- ❏ writing poems, litanies, scripts
- ❏ completing sentences
- ❏ keeping a journal
- ❏ learning new words
- ❏ answering questions
- ❏ discussing
- ❏ playing word games

Cautions: This learner becomes frustrated when there's no verbal stimulation.

Logical/Mathematical

In a nutshell: This learner is a questioner and loves abstract and scientific thinking, numbers, categories, and patterns.

Learns best by: This learner learns best by asking and answering questions, categorizing and classifying things

Activities:

- ❏ solving number problems
- ❏ solving word puzzles
- ❏ conducting experiments
- ❏ working with numbers and math
- ❏ problem solving
- ❏ exploring patterns and relationships
- ❏ following step-by-step explanations
- ❏ deciphering and creating codes
- ❏ scientific observation and drawing conclusions

Cautions:
This learner
finds it difficult to
function in
arenas of
confusion.

O TASTE AND SEE THAT THE LORD IS GOOD

Musical/Rhythmic

In a nutshell: This learner enjoys using music, songs, and patterns in a rhythm.

Learns best by: This learner learns best by using rhythm, melody, and music combined with information.

Activities:

- ❏ singing, humming, and listening to music
- ❏ writing songs or writing new words to familiar tunes
- ❏ making and playing musical instruments
- ❏ responding to music
- ❏ learning Bible verses set to music or rhythm
- ❏ listening and learning story songs
- ❏ rapping (listening to and writing)
- ❏ learning hymns
- ❏ rhythm games

Cautions: To this learner, lectures are boring.

Visual Spatial

In a nutshell: This learner enjoys visualizing and creating mental images, manipulating shapes and objects. This learner has a sense of sight and an ability to visualize objects and create mental images.

Learns best by: This learner learns best by visualizing and dreaming about concepts and ideas

Activities:

- ❏ drawing

- ❏ art activities using various media

- ❏ designing and building models

- ❏ looking at pictures

- ❏ watching videos

- ❏ working mazes

- ❏ putting together puzzles

- ❏ using maps, charts, posters, diagrams

- ❏ guided imagery

Cautions: This learner is discouraged by too much printed material.

O TASTE AND SEE THAT THE LORD IS GOOD

Body/Kinesthetic

In a nutshell: This learner enjoys physical movement, knowing wisdom of the body, enjoys bodily motion.

Learns best by: This learner learns best by physically becoming involved with the information in some way

Activities:

- ❏ physical activities and active games
- ❏ role playing, pantomime, and drama
- ❏ motions to songs and prayers
- ❏ freeze frame stories
- ❏ finger plays
- ❏ crafts
- ❏ moving and dancing
- ❏ touching objects
- ❏ marching, waving streamers

Cautions: This learner often "tunes out" during long periods of inactivity.

Intrapersonal

In a nutshell: This learner enjoys the inner states of being, self-reflection, awareness of spiritual realities.

Learns best by: This learner learns best by working alone on projects.

Activities:

- ❏ working alone
- ❏ focusing on inner feelings
- ❏ identifying with characters in a story
- ❏ prayer
- ❏ meditation
- ❏ independent research
- ❏ journaling

Cautions: This learner often withdraws during group activities.

Interpersonal

In a nutshell: This learner enjoys person-to-person relationships and communications.

Learns best by: This learner learns best by talking with others.

Activities:

- ❏ working in small groups

- ❏ comparing and contrasting ideas with others

- ❏ interviewing, discussing, and dialoguing

- ❏ answering questions

- ❏ playing cooperative learning games

- ❏ brainstorming ideas

- ❏ asking and answering questions

- ❏ planning and attending parties and celebrations

- ❏ participating in service projects

Cautions: This learner is stifled by long periods of independent study.

Total

Verbal/Linguistic   _____

Logical/Mathematical   _____

Visual/Spatial   _____

Body/Kinesthetic   _____

Musical/Rhythmic   _____

Interpersonal   _____

Intrapersonal   _____

In which category did you find the most activities that appealed to you?_____

Was there more than one?_____

In which category did you make the fewest check marks? _____

On the next page write the names of each of the children in your class. Observe them carefully for the next few weeks. What is the preferred learning style for each child? Are there some activities that most of the children enjoy? Are there some activities that no one responds to very well? Are there learning activities that you have never used? What changes could you make?

All God's Children Have Style

Child's Name	Preferred Learning Style

Child's Name	Preferred Learning Style

O TASTE AND SEE THAT THE LORD IS GOOD

Some Practical Helps

O TASTE AND SEE THAT THE LORD IS GOOD

Bringing Bible Stories to Life

by Ann David

"Miss Ann, tell me again why he climbed up that tree," asked four-year-old Maddie.

I paused for a minute. I could try to answer the question and explain that Zacchaeus was trying to see over the heads of the crowd, or I could repeat the whole story again. It was obvious that Maddie, and perhaps others in the class, hadn't quite understood the Bible story.

And then an idea came to me. I asked Maddie to kneel down on the floor with the rest of the class standing all around her. I started to tell the story again. Maddie complained that she couldn't see me. So then I had her stand on a sturdy chair so that her head was above the rest of the class, still standing around her.

I continued on with the story pausing a couple of times to ask Maddie if she could still see me all right. Maddie suddenly understood why Zacchaeus wanted to climb up in a tree—to better see Jesus. Because Maddie had been able to put herself into the experience that Zacchaeus had been in, the Bible story had come to life for her.

Of course all the other children then wanted to be Zacchaeus too, so we spent the rest of the class repeating the scene. But at the end of the class, they

all really understood why Zacchaeus had climbed up that sycamore tree.

Children often need to put themselves in a story to better understand it. Participating in drama will help make the story more meaningful and more real.

There are several types of dramatic experiences that can be used in the Sunday school classroom. My favorites are interactive group experiences, news interview shows, and dramatizations of the Bible story. These can often be found in the curriculum offerings for each quarter.

Interactive Group Experiences

This drama experience allows the entire class to participate and is wonderful for preschool and early elementary children. To begin, make sure you, as the leader, are familiar with the Bible story. As you read the story, try to imagine the scene using all of your senses. What do you want the children to see, hear, feel, smell, or taste during the experience?

For instance, in the story "Jesus Calms the Storm," you might want the children to see the dramatic changes in weather, hear the sounds of the storm, and feel the spray of the water. Then build the drama from those sensory images.

Ask the children how it felt to be in the storm. For the children playing the disciples, did the sounds of the storm make them feel afraid? What did they feel when they saw Jesus stop the wind and the waves? For the children playing the storm, were they amazed that Jesus could stop them?

News Interview Shows
This is an exciting way to involve middle and older elementary children in a Bible story. This approach works great with dramatizing the miracles of Jesus. Once again make sure you, as the leader, are familiar with the Bible story. As you read the story, consider the characters who are involved. What happens in the story, and who does it happen to? Who are the witnesses to the event?

It is fun to consider the animals or inanimate objects involved in "The Net Full of Fish," the fish might have something to say about suddenly being caught in the net: "I was trying hard to swim away from that net, but somehow I was pulled against my will towards it." Or in "The Wedding at Cana," the water that became wine might say: "Hey, I was just sitting around in this pot, perfectly content to be H$_2$O, when someone named Jesus was called to the scene."

The news interview show can be presented either as an "in-studio" production, with the interviewer seated at a table or desk and the guests sitting next to him or her, or done "on location" with the interviewer talking to participants at the site of the event. In either situation, have the person playing the interviewer ask each character questions about what happened in the story.

At the end of the show, talk about the miracle. Did all of the participants realize what had happened? Did they believe it? Did they understand that it was Jesus who turned the water into wine? What do you think the disciples and wedding guests were feeling about Jesus, both before and after the miracle?

50

Dramatization of the Bible Story

Older elementary children will find it fun and meaningful to actually write out and rehearse a scene. Ask the children to read a specific Bible story and write it out as a script. Encourage them to use their imaginations to paraphrase the dialogue. If you are working with a large class, split the children up into several groups, each working with the same story. It will be interesting to see how the different groups will present the scene.

Allow plenty of time to write and rehearse the script. Have the children think about the setting for the scene. Do they need any furniture or props? Simple costumes can be added to help with characterizations. With an old pillowcase, cut holes for the arms and head. Or take a yard of striped or textured fabric, or an old towel; fold it in half, and cut a hole for the head. Tie rope or cording around the waist for a belt. A simple biblical-type costume can help a child feel more like Zacchaeus or Jesus.

When ready, have the children perform their scene with props and costumes. After the dramatization, ask Jesus how it felt to be teaching from a boat in the lake. What was Simon Peter thinking as he was first pulling nets out of the water? What were his thoughts when he saw all the fish in the nets? How did James and John feel when Simon called them to help with the nets? What does Jesus mean that Simon will now be catching people?

With all age groups and with all three of these drama types, remember the process is more important than the final product. But for an older class to really get involved with a news interview show or dramatization, videotape the interviews or scenes, and watch them later as a class with popcorn and lemonade for a special treat. Or invite another class or even parents to be an audience. Watching a drama performance can also bring a Bible story to life.

Maddie might have understood the story of Zacchaeus if she had seen it acted out. But I'm sure she would have responded as the other children did in my class: "When can I climb the tree?" "When can I be Zacchaeus?"

Adapted from *Children's Teacher*, Vol. 8, No. 4, © 2001 Cokesbury.

Sing a New Song

by Linda Ray Miller

One of my favorite childhood memories of Sunday school was singing songs. I could belt out "Jesus Love Me" and "Jesus Loves the Little Children" with the best of them. I learned Bible stories by singing "Only a Boy Named David" and "Zacchaeus Was a Wee Little Man." To this day when I am looking for a Scripture passage in the New Testament, I sing the books of the New Testament to a tune I learned in the fifth grade.

Now, however, many children come to Sunday school and never hear or sing songs. Perhaps the teacher has other activities for the children to do, or maybe the teacher doesn't feel comfortable using music in the classroom. Whatever the reason, some children are not experiencing the fun of learning about God through music.

How can music teach children about God?

Just as some children learn better when ideas are presented to them visually, others learn best when ideas are presented to them aurally, especially through music. Music is a great teaching tool because it reinforces the learning experience with:

- **Repetition—**Repeating songs again and again helps children learn Bible verses, stories, and facts.

- **Movement—**Children are more apt to retain things they have learned with their whole bodies. Singing and moving to music involves the whole child in ways that sitting and listening cannot.

- **Fun—**Music is just plain fun! We want our children to want to come to Sunday school. And we know that children love music. What an easy way to incorporate fun activities that can also teach!

52

Even the most non-musical teacher can include music in the classroom. Every lesson incorporates music into the lesson plan, offering lots of songs that are fun to sing and listen to. Create opportunities for adding music to your children's Sunday school experience.

Musical Possibilities:
- Play music as the children enter the classroom and while the children are working on craft activities or at centers.

- Make a music listening center from a large appliance box filled with pillows, cassette or CD player, and headphones. Use the cassette or CD that accompanies your curriculum, or have a church musician or youth group make a tape of a single song that you would like the children to learn.

For non-readers, place a green sticker on the "Play" button, and a red sticker on the "Stop" button, and a yellow sticker on the "Rewind" button. Teach the children to put on the headphones, push the green button to listen, the red button to stop, and the yellow button to rewind the tape before leaving the center. This will quickly become one of your most popular centers.

- Use music as a signal for transitions. Singing a song is a gentler reminder that it is time to put toys and materials away than the use of verbal instructions. Some songs tend to build excitement for active learning times, and some are better for preparing children for quieter, more meditative activities.

- Call children to worship with music. Use the same song each week to begin your worship time. Invite the children to sing along or just listen to the music.

- Invite the children to move to the music. Ask the children to move in the way the music makes them feel. For smooth, flowing music, give the children scarves or crepe paper streamers. For music with a heavy rhythm, have the children march or play rhythm instruments. Ask the children to show with their bodies what feeling or emotion the music evokes.

Directed dances such as the "Hokey Pokey" are always a lot of fun for children. Use "If You're Happy and You Know It" to gain the attention of an entire class quickly.

- Personalize the music part of the learning experience. Record your church's youth choir singing this quarter's songs using the Songbook

and the Cassette/CD. Put the recording in the listening center. Children love to recognize an older sibling's voice on a cassette. Another option is to record your own class singing the songs.

- Use motion to help children memorize words to longer songs. Often when given a little encouragement, children will make up their own motions. The use of sign language for repetitive phrases is often a part of the curriculum and encourages appreciation of those who must use signs to speak.

- The best way to learn a song is to simply sing it a lot! When teaching a new song, have the children listen as you say the words in rhythm. Ask the children to repeat the words only. The next week invite the children to listen as you sing or play the song several times and encourage the children to sing along. By the third week, you may have children requesting the song or you may hear them singing it as they work on their art projects.

Whatever you do, give the children in your class the opportunity to experience some musical fun this quarter. Use music to teach your class about the love of God. In the process, you might just create some musical memories of your own.

From *Children's Teacher, Vol. 8, No. 1, Fall 2000,* © 2000 Cokesbury.

O TASTE AND SEE THAT THE LORD IS GOOD

Dancing Before the Lord

by Beth Teegarden

Peek inside a children's play area and what do you see? Children jumping, running, skipping, turning, rolling, bending, kneeling, and just about any body movement that can be done. Children love to move and be active. They love to express themselves with their hands, arms, and legs. It only seems natural they would like to dance. Dance is defined as "a series of rhythmical motions and steps." In an unorganized way the children are already dancing. They just need an "organizer." Being the organizer is not difficult and using the following suggestions, you can organize these energetic children into dancers.

Why dance?

Dance is not new to our religious belief. David was "dancing before the Lord" all the time (2 Samuel 6:14; 1 Chronicles 15:29; Psalm 30:11). Dancing was a way for the people to rejoice and praise God. Today we can follow the ways of the Israelites and "Praise him with tambourine and dance." (Psalm 150:4)

Dancing and moving is also a way for children to express their feelings. Many times children may not be able to adequately say how they feel about God, but ask a child to show you how he or she feels, and you will quickly get the picture. We need to give our children this opportunity in church.

Dancing and moving is also a wonderful teaching tool. When we move, we feel, and when we feel, we remember, and when we remember, we learn. Dancing helps us do this.

What Can You Dance To?

If you're going to dance, you must have music, right? Yes and no.

By all means, music is beautiful to dance with. Children's music is generally very descriptive and easy to choreograph. You could try looking for songs in the curriculum, the hymnal, children's songbooks, Bible school songs, praise choruses, folk tunes, and children's

choir anthems. Most music found in these sources will be easy for the children to learn, and some may even have movement suggestions with the music.

But, music is not the only source for dance. The spoken word can be enhanced with the use of movement. A litany, a prayer, a Psalm, a Scripture reading, or a Bible story could all become more visual with the use of dance. Many of the same sources for music will also have prayers and litanies in them and of course, the hymnal and Bible will be of use. You may also be adventurous and try writing your own or let the children work together and write something they would want to dance to.

Creating the Dance

You may think this is what you can't do, but with patience and imagination you will be able to create a dance. The first thing you will want to do is take whatever you are going to dance to and look for given words. These are words that tell you what to do. For example: kneel, clap hands, stand, turn around, pray,

jump for joy, and so on. If possible, include the actions these words describe in your dance. The next thing you will want to do is visualize the other words of the song or text. Ask yourself, "What do I see when we say praise or world or baby or people or stable?" This will give you visual ideas of the pictures you are trying to make.

Finally, you will want to decide what you want the dance to communicate. What is the message? When you decide this, make sure all the movements and pictures you have created are communicating the message. Put all of this together, and you have a dance.

Can All Ages Dance?

Absolutely! The only thing you need to be careful about is age-appropriate movements. You want the children to be able to enjoy what they are doing and not become frustrated with the dance. A good motto to keep in mind is "the simpler the better." This will make the dance easier to create, easier to teach, easier to learn, and more usable in the classroom.

Preschool and younger elementary children have a hard time accomplishing movements that involve using two or more large motor skills at the same time. They would have difficulty moving their arms up and down while marching in place. On the other hand, they could do both of these movements if done separately. This age will also have difficulty doing partner or group movements. Holding hands and walking in a circle is a good group movement for this age but anything harder will be frustrating.

O TASTE AND SEE THAT THE LORD IS GOOD

Older elementary children can probably accomplish most anything you would want to do. They will welcome a challenge and would most likely want to help create the dance. Some children may be shy about moving at first, but with encouragement and a loving atmosphere within the group, these children will begin to feel more comfortable.

When and Where?
A great time to begin a dance is when a season of the liturgical year changes. In the later part of November, you could create a dance that could be used during the Advent season. This way the children can really learn the dance well and get to do the dance more than once or twice. As the liturgical season changes, you could then change to a different dance. To begin with you might want to just incorporate dance into your classroom setting as part of your lesson. You could spend a small amount of class time each week to teach parts of the dance, and once the dance is learned, you could then use it for several weeks in the worship section of your lesson. After this is accomplished, you may

want to do the dance for other classes in the church, at children's worship, or even during Sunday worship services. Another great opportunity to use dance is Vacation Bible School. Since the children meet each day, you can easily teach them movements to the songs, stories, or theme of Vacation Bible School. This could be a rare opportunity when all ages of children could learn the same dance and do it together.

Other places you could incorporate dance would be day school and day care, church picnics, church camp, retreats, confirmation and special programs like Christmas and Easter.

Above all, it is important to remember that dance is just another way we can worship God. Teach your dancers that they are not performing a dance for entertainment, but are showing praise to God with movement of their bodies. With this kind of attitude, each and every time we dance we are truly "dancing before the Lord."

From *Children's Teacher, Vol. 6, No. 1, Fall, 1998,* © 1998 Cokesbury.

Teaching Children to Pray

by Cecile Adams

Chris, a first grader, talked with his teacher about going to his grandfather's funeral. He spoke of being sad when standing by the grave. "What did you do, Chris?" asked the teacher?

"I said a prayer," replied Chris softly.

"I'm glad you did. You can talk with God anytime, anywhere, about anything," said the teacher.

Anna sat at the kitchen table with her grandchildren. Mark and Mandy—fifth grade twins. Another member of the church had just called to tell Anna that a friend of theirs was fired from her job. Anna asked Mark and Mandy to pray with her for the friend.

"You mean you want us to ask God to find her another job?" asked Mark.

"No," replied Anna. "I want to ask God to help us know how to support her in this difficult time. I want to ask God to provide for her what she needs and to let God know that I am willing to be part of what God provides. What else do you think we might include in our prayer?"

For the third time in one night, Samuel came to Eli's bed and said, "Here I am, for you called me."

Twice Eli, the priest had told Samuel to go back to sleep, for he had not called. This time Eli paid attention. Though a word from God was rare in those days, perhaps God was calling Samuel. Eli instructed Samuel, "Go, lie down; and if he calls you, you shall say, 'Speak, Lord , for your servant is listening'" (as found in 1 Samuel 3).

The story does not end there, for God was indeed calling Samuel to give him quite a message to deliver to Eli. The news was not good: Eli's sons had blasphemed God and would be punished. Samuel was reluctant to give the message to Eli, but at Eli's insistence, told him all that God had said.

Our children do have a relationship with God. Often what they need from us is help in recognizing God's presence and words to say in response. Like Eli, we may be slow in recognizing what is happening.

Our responsibility and opportunity is not so much to teach our children how to pray, but to join them in praying and to learn from their alertness and

O TASTE AND SEE THAT THE LORD IS GOOD

spontaneity. To do that well, we must be prayerful ourselves. We must be in a current relationship with God.

About Praying

These questions may be helpful as you think about your own prayer life. When do you pray? What do you pray about? What does God say to you? Do you pray for people you don't like, not to change them but to be more loving toward them? When have your children or your students heard you pray? When have you asked your children or your students to pray with you? How have your prayers changed in the last five years?

As you think about these questions and your answers, you can join the children in your life in prayer.

Times for Prayer

Times for Prayer

Some times for praying with children are:
  planned worship in your classroom
  at snack and mealtimes
  at nap and bedtime
  on birthdays
  as the seasons change
  watching a sunset
  in the middle of an argument
  when a new brother or sister is born
  when someone moves away
  when someone new moves in
  when you or they don't know what to do
  when choosing a gift
  before going to school
  in the midst of a storm
  when something beautiful happens
     unexpectedly
  when someone dies
  on Christmas Day
  washing the dishes
  putting away toys
  bandaging a cut
  deciding how to spend an allowance
  anytime

Kinds of prayers

Some kinds of prayer are:
  giving thanks
  talking with God about wants or
  needs
  sharing feelings with God
  talking with God about someone else
  listening to God
  spontaneously doing something good
  for someone else

Prayer Postures

Some prayer postures are:
  head bowed, eyes closed
  eyes open, looking at one another
  moving to music
  holding hands
  lying down
  hugging yourself, someone else,
    or a whole group of persons
  head up, hands lifted up
  singing
  sitting
  walking or running
  on your knees
  playing a music instrument

Adapted from *Children's Teacher, Vol. 2, no. 1*, © 1994 Cokesbury.

O TASTE AND SEE THAT THE LORD IS GOOD

Cut, Paste, Paint, Sculpt— Using the Visual Arts

by LeeDell Stickler

Visual arts (or art experiences) are all those activities that many children love most and teachers often avoid. They are usually messier than the regular paper and pencil variety of activities. They usually involve more supplies and consequently more clean-up time. But visual arts appeal to more than one learning style.

Many teachers leave out art experiences because they feel that their time in Sunday school is so short that to waste it on "crafts" serves no purpose. They proclaim, "Let the school systems teach art. We're concerned with the Bible." But, in the past few years the school system has had similar thoughts and dropped art from its curriculum. But as a teacher, you probably already know the value of art as a teaching medium.

In choosing art experiences, keep these things in mind.

✄ The art project should be worthwhile, not just something to keep the children busy.
✄ The art project should teach important skills.
✄ The art project should directly relate to the theme of the lesson.

1. **The visual arts are an effective teaching tool.** Long ago, churches used visual arts—stained glass windows, paintings, and sculpture—to communicate Bible stories to the believers. These people were basically illiterate and unable to read the Bible for themselves. Most of our children can read, but as teachers we already have learned that children learn visually much faster than they do auditorily. Visual arts increase the impact of the Bible stories.

2. **Art experiences involve all of the senses.** Not only are the children using their eyes, but they are also using their hands, their noses, and their ears. Some art projects even involve the sense of taste—that is if they can eat it. A child is a walking mass of perception. One of

our tasks is to keep this perception open and growing.

3. **Art experiences develop the individual creativity.** We are created in God's image. What a wonderful gift! Therefore, art experiences should celebrate our individuality. Being creative, however, does not automatically mean a child is a born artist or that this is their preferred learning style. Make this one part of the total experience. Developing our God-given creativity means developing an awareness of ideas, feelings, experiences—a special way of learning, thinking, and perceiving. Most children have the potential of being creative, provided they are given the opportunity to explore this gift.

4. **Art experiences teach skills of community living, skills learned only through experiences.** This appeals to the interpersonal learner. The Bible speaks of how wonderful it is for God's people to live together in harmony. Art experiences help teach some of the skills necessary for this harmony—patience, flexibility, willingness to share, conservation of resources, cooperation, and acceptance.

5. **Art experiences develop fine-motor skills.** Children learn to cut by cutting, to draw by drawing. Provide these experiences in a non-threatening, noncompetitive, relaxed atmosphere where each child is valued for his or her individual contribution. Keep these points in mind as you introduce the visual arts into your teaching ministry:

- Relate the activity directly to the lesson. If a craft is only a craft then the time might be better spent doing something else.

- Time is an important factor. Most teacher books give an estimated amount of time each activity will consume. But remember, this is only an average.

- Encourage creativity. The assembly line project soon will get tossed into the trash can as it is not really the child's "project." Not everyone's project has to look exactly like the picture in the teacher book. Sometimes it is more fun to choose an alternative way of doing the craft as well. Add your own imagination.

- Make sure the art project is appropriate for your children's abilities. A project may be appropriate to the average age and grade level you are teaching, but it may not be appropri-

ate for your children. In all projects, consider the children you teach.

- Do not discount a project because you don't have the supplies, the space, or the time. Consider alternatives. Is there another way to do the project? Are there pre-class things you can do to shave time from the project? Are there other supplies you can substitute?

- Make clean up an integral part of the project. Children should learn to be responsible for their own "space." This includes maintaining it before, during, and after they are there.

The visual arts is a vital part of experiential learning. It uses all the senses and it touches more than just one learning style. The visual arts tap the unique individuality present in each child.

Cooperative Learning Makes Sense
by LeeDell Stickler

Cooperative learning is more than games and activities in contrived groups. Cooperative learning is an attitude of respect for the children's capacity to learn, to teach and to contribute to the entire learning situation. Children who learn in this kind of an environment take the first steps to becoming lifelong learners because they experience ownership, initiative, and motivation to learn.

It is natural for people to work together. When trying to decide whether cooperative learning activities are right for you and your class, ask yourself these questions:

Do children learn best in a quiet, isolated environment?

Why do children come to Sunday school? What are their goals?

Should children be involved in each other's learning?

Can student motivation have an effect on the problems associated with group process?

A Case for Cooperative Learning

As teachers we are aware that children learn in a variety of ways and under a variety of conditions. Before any formal

training ever began in a child's life, he or she learned a little something from everyone they met along the way. They generally learned the most from the people they liked the most.

For example, take learning to talk. Most children are expected to just "pick it up." The complicated syntax of language is learned without a grammar lesson. Children learn to say, "I like to hear stories from the Bible" instead of "Hear I like from the Bible stories." They learn

O TASTE AND SEE THAT THE LORD IS GOOD

this very well, even though the techniques we use are very disorganized.

Here is what we know about children and the way they learn:
• Children are involved with a variety of people, and through that interaction they learn. In isolation, children cannot learn.

• Children have a tolerance for being immersed in something. They thrive in environments with lots of stimulation.

• Children have an internal motivator that helps them want to learn. They will fall repeatedly and still learn to walk and will struggle to communicate their needs through repeated requests.

• Children are familiar with learning from a variety of individuals. They learn from siblings, family, neighbors, and friends.

• Children are capable of learning without being taught the breakdown of individual skills.

• Children have their own intrinsic purpose which is to learn.

Teachers cannot pour knowledge into children's ears. If the students are not ready to receive information, then it will not be passed on.

Through cooperative learning the children will discover the difference between teaching and telling. Telling is giving someone the answer. Teaching is helping someone find the answer.

What Is Cooperative Learning?
• Cooperative learning is a teaching strategy that involves children of all performance levels working together in small groups to reach a common goal. This process of working toward a goal may be one of the most valuable elements to a child's development of social skills.

• Cooperative learning increases motivation to learn by adding variety to teaching methods.

• Cooperative learning allows for different learning styles and performance levels to be accommodated.

• Cooperative learning creates opportunities for the exchange of more and better ideas rather than working alone or competitively.

But one thing to keep in mind, Cooperative learning requires careful planning, organization, and teacher interaction.

Why Use Cooperative Learning?
Children learn best when allowed to interact positively with others in their environment. Cooperative learning provides experiences that develop language skills, thinking and problem solving skills, social skills as well as academic skills.

Many children that we identify as behavior problems or children with attention deficit disorder are still full of curiosity and want to learn. Cooperative learning establishes better discipline and encourages children to want to learn new things. Besides Cooperative learning provides direct experiences that allow positive interaction of children and learning.

How Do I Introduce Cooperative Learning to My Class?

1. Group Size
The size of the group is determined by the teacher after selecting the content for the lesson. Groups can be two to five or even six, depending on the activity. Groups can also encompass the entire classroom full of children. The teacher will need to take careful stock of the activity and decide how that group will work together.

2. Group Make-up
Cooperative learning activities can make children feel a part of the class and reduce discipline. A mixed group of performance levels, reading levels, gender, and ethnic background works best. Children may be denied valuable lessons if they are always grouped with children of similar temperament. Some children have difficult times with groups. They may be reticent or overly bossy. But if they are never given the opportunity to learn, who will teach them?

3. Group Assignments
Many activities lend themselves to working together in small groups. Make sure each child has a job to do and that each child understands the task at hand.

4. Classroom Setup
The teacher must be able to move within and around the cooperative learning groups to provide guidance when and if it is needed.

5. Group Monitoring
The teacher should monitor how the children are working together, as well as the product being constructed or the task being completed. The teacher should be observant and praise children for good behavior and good performance and encourage them to continue to work and be cooperative.

6. Behavior Management
Expectations of behavior should be set and consistent within the classroom. Keep the rules simple: use quiet voices, stay at your workplace, work together, help one another, and say nice words to others.

7. Peer Teaching
The value of peer teaching cannot be stressed enough. These kinds of activities build lasting friendships and demonstrate for the children the enjoyment of working with someone else to solve problems. This is a life skill that can only be taught by experiencing it.

8. Sharing Time
It is critical to bring the boys and girls together at the end of a cooperative learning activity to bring closure to the lesson. Children are asked to share experiences and products with children from other groups. If your group is small and you only have one group, allow them to share what they learn.

A Sample Cooperative Learning Activity for Younger Children

You will need: a dish pan filled half full of water, a tray of items, a sheet of aluminum foil, a piece of clay, a small rock and a paper clip.

Read the children the story of Noah's ark up to the point of verse 22. (Genesis 5:9-22) For younger children it might be better to use a Noah's ark storybook.

Ask: What did God want Noah to do? (build a boat) What was going to go into the boat? (all the animals, two of each kind) What was going to happen? (God was going to flood the earth.)

Give the children the task of trying to decide which items on the tray would sink if caught in the flood and which items would float. Place all the "floaters" on the right side and all the "sinkers" on the left side. Then challenge the teams to come up with a way so that the rock and the paper clip will float on top of the water. **One possible solution:** Create a boat from the sheet of aluminum foil and place the rock and paper clip inside.

Debrief: Talk about the kind of boat that Noah built and the size it would have been to carry all the animals and still float.

A Sample Cooperative Learning Activity for Older Children

You will need: twenty index cards, two business sized envelopes, felt-tip markers.

On the first ten index cards, write the Bible verse (Genesis 1:1), one word on each card: In, the, beginning, God, created, the, heavens, and, the, earth. Mix them up and place them in an envelope labeled "Word Cards."

On the next ten index cards, write the ten clues, one on each card.

• The last word in the Bible verse is the word we use to identify the third planet from the sun. (earth)

• The fourth word in the Bible verse is our version of the Hebrew word Yahweh. (God)

• The eighth word in the Bible verse is a connector word, used to join two other words. (and)

• The third word in the Bible verse means the opposite of the word "ending." (beginning)

• The fifth word in the Bible verse means "to make something." (created)

• The ninth word in the Bible verse is the same as the second word and the sixth word. (the)

• The first word in the Bible verse means the opposite of the word "out." (In)

• The seventh word in the Bible verse refers to the part of the universe that is beyond the earth. (heavens)

• The second word in the Bible verse rhymes with the word "see." (the)

• The sixth word of the Bible verse is the same word as the second and the ninth word. (the)

Instructions to the groups: In each team you have the clues that will help you put the Bible verse in order. Deal out the clue cards. Each person must have at least one clue card. But it doesn't have to be even. Spread the word cards out on the floor or table. Then in turn each participant will read his or her clue. The team will then work together to put the Bible verse in order using the clues. The person who has the clue must be the person to read it.

Puzzles, Mazes, and Word Finds

by LeeDell Stickler

Every class has one. They are easily recognizable. They are the children who, when given a choice of activities, immediately go to the puzzles. The puzzles can be manipulatives, or cards, or crosswords, or word finds. But these activities are magnets attracting the logical mathematical child.

Many creative teachers shun the activities they find on paper. These dot-to-dots, mazes, and decoding activities appear to be only "busy work" for the teacher who is unprepared or who is much more creative than that. So the creative teacher often relegates these puzzles, and mazes, and word finds to the last resort category, only to be used when there is extra time but not enough extra time to do something more creative. What this teacher often forgets is that there are children in their classes for whom this is the preferred learning style. These children thrive on figuring out the strategies and discovering the answers, even to a paper and pencil activity. These children are your logical mathematical learners.

Characteristics of the Logical Mathematical Child

The logical mathematical child has the ability to use reason, logic, and numbers effectively. Even at the preschool age level, these learners think conceptually in patterns. (That's the toddler who is always taking apart her or his toys, and once they've figured out how it works, they are no longer interested.) These children make connections between pieces of information and make sense out of seemingly unrelated pieces. The logical mathematical child is curious about the world around them. They want to know "why" something is the way it is or "how" something works.

They always ask lots of questions and like to do experiments. These are the children who are willing to spend the time to discover the answers.

• The number smart child thrives on problem solving. Give them a question or a challenge where the answer is unknown or the solution to the problem is undeterminable, and they are ready to go—and hate being interrupted before the solution is found.

• The number smart child also likes classifying and categorizing information, working with abstract concepts to figure out the reationship of items to each other. Just give a logical mathematical child a tray of unmatched buttons and watch what happens.

• The number smart child likes handling long chains of reason to make logical progressions.

• The number smart child loves doing controlled experiments, questioning and wondering about natural events. What would happen if it didn't rain? What would happen if the sun didn't shine?

• The number smart child loves performing complex mathematical calculations. If Mary and Joseph could walk thirty miles a day. How long would the trip from Nazareth to Bethlehem take?

• The number smart child loves working with geometric shapes. Tangrams are a particular challenge for this child. Let them try to discover how the pyramids were built.

Activities for Preschoolers

putting together puzzles
sorting and categorizing objects
imagining the whole from a
    portion of a picture
discovering what happens when
simple mazes and follow the
    dots
matching things that go
    together
finding the hidden pictures
finding what's different
simple cooking and mixing
stringing beads

Activities for Younger Elementary

dot-to dot puzzles (under 50)
assembling puzzles
making connections between
    unrelated objects
exploring the natural world
simple decoding puzzles
simple crossword puzzles
simple wordfinds (not backward)
complicated mazes
building projects
solving simulated problems
following recipes and cooking
sequencing

Activities for Older Elementary

timelines
episodic sequencing
more complicated mazes
dot-to-dot puzzles (80-100 dots)
anagrams
word scrambles
mirror reflections
tangrams
crossword puzzles
decoding puzzles
controlled scientific experiments
mathematical problems
drawing conclusions from pieces
of data
mapping and graphing
creating quizzes
synonyms and antonyms
word jumbles
how to get from here to there
visual puzzles

O TASTE AND SEE THAT THE LORD IS GOOD

Game for a Game?

by LeeDell Stickler

For goodness sakes, we're in church. The children shouldn't be playing games, they should be learning about God, and Jesus, and the Bible. Games don't have a place here, do they?

Games offer excitement, challenge, and a natural platform for skill and content acquisition. The safe setting of a game offers children the opportunity to use their ingenuity and confront childhood concerns. Games encourage children to participate, explore, communicate, challenge themselves, develop healthy attitudes, build confidence in the abilities. Besides games are just plain fun! Studies suggest that active children have higher self-esteem and a greater independence and experience less stress. Games nurture the whole child-body, intellect, emotion, and spirit—allowing learning and child development to take place in a spontaneous natural manner. Besides, some children simply need to move and games provide a natural outlet for this movement.

Games allow children to:
• engage in healthy alternatives to less stimulating activities
• focus and channel energy
• develop socially, emotionally, intellectually, and physically
• develop skills of concentration, memory, creativity, problem solving and decision making
• build bonds of communication and friendship
• explore physical activities and enhance athletic abilities
• build independence, self-esteem, and confidence
• learn to handle healthy competition
• strive to do their best and appreciate their capabilities and limitations
• learn to appreciate the capabilities and limitations of others
• exercise their whole being: body, mind, and spirit
• learn to play for the sake of play.

Dealing with Competition
Games should be fun. Through games children will learn about fair play, teamwork, personal success and having fun. But we spend a great deal of time in Sunday school teaching the children that we should work together and that God loves everyone equally. So what do you do about games where one team sees itself as a "loser." Try to find as many cooperative games as you can competitive games. Children will never go through life not having to compete. But a variety of games will provide the different physical, social, and cognitive abilities of the children who are playing.

Cooperative games teach children to value the efforts of one another, assist and encourage one another, understand that working together is important and enjoyable, and learn that games are fun without the competitive challenge. For younger children no-lose games are generally better choices.

Competitive games allow children to test themselves against their peers, set goals, test and challenge themselves. These games present lessons in handling victory of loss in a sense of fun. As a teacher, if your class is highly competitive, your better choices will be cooperative games as well.

Choosing Game Leaders

When choosing game leaders, look for children who model and value fair play. The right leader in a game can tone down rivalries, avoid acceptance rejection concepts, and praise accomplishments, efforts and responsible behavior. The right game leader will demonstrate enthusiasm, teamwork, cooperation, respect for the other players, and the joy of playing.

Setting the Rules

When you are choosing the games, remember the age level of children who will be playing. Some children are just beginning to develop their large motor skills and the games need to require little more than running, jumping, hopping, and so forth. Too many directions will make it impossible to play. For an older group of children keep in mind that they are just beginning to develop their many social and emotional skills. In the excitement of a game children may forget the basic rules of conduct, safety concerns and social niceties. Gentle reminders and role modeling are necessary tools for the game leader. Keep the rules simple and easy to understand.

Providing a Safe Play Area

Obviously most churches have limited space to play

games unless you have gathered in a fellowship hall or an outdoor play area. If the game may lend itself to noise, your best bet would be to go outside, weather permitting.

Wherever you go to play the games, make sure that the area is safe. There should be no sharp objects within the play area. Push all chairs, tables and furniture back against the wall if the game is active. Go over the game rules carefully before commencing play, reinforcing the fact that the children are not to heckle other participants and that what's fair or not will be established before the game begins.

From the beginning of time children have played games. Throughout the ages and around the world, games have changed very little. Many games originated from an imitation of adult behaviors. Down through time, the only alterations have been those that reflect our modern times. Games are even generally passed on by parents, grandparents, and often by other children.

O TASTE AND SEE THAT THE LORD IS GOOD

Some Games to Play

With Preschoolers

Move to the Mailbox

This game is used with the story of Paul and how he wrote letters to the church at Corinth. You will need a mailbox or a box that can be used as a mailbox. Set the mailbox in an open space in the classroom. Give each child an envelope or a folded sheet of paper. Gather the children in a group across the room from the mailbox. Have the children pretend that where they are standing is their home and that they all have letters to mail. Tell each of the children how to move to the mailbox where they will mail their letters and then tell them how to move back home. When anyone drops a letter in the mailbox, have the children say the Bible verse: "Love never ends." Give instructions to the children such as: Wanda, hop to the mailbox and mail your letter. Wanda, gallop back home. Billy, slide to the box and mail your letter. Billy, tiptoe back home.

Play a Matching Game

Put out a set of matching cards, either commercial ones, ones provided by the curriculum, or ones that you have made. Let the children enjoy finding the cards that match.

Steppin' Out

This activity is used with the story of Hannah and baby Samuel. Have the children move to one side of the room. Use masking tape to make a goal line on the other side of the room. Tell the children the story of Hannah and how God answered her prayer. Say that Samuel grew, just like them. When they were babies, they took baby steps, now they can take giant steps. Play music. Have the children take giant steps toward the line. Stop the music. When the music stops the children will take baby steps toward the line. Alternate until all the children get to the line.

With Kindergarten and Younger Elementary

Play a Mirror Game

When we try to follow Jesus' rule to do to others as we would have them do to us, we sometimes have to imagine that we are the other persons in order to think about what those persons might want us to do for them. We can play a silly game to pretend that we are other persons.

Pair up the children and have the partners face each other. Designate one partner in each pair as the leader. Explain that the leaders must stand in one place but that they may move their arms, heads, and bodies in any way they want. Tell the persons who are facing the leaders to move their arms, heads, and bodies to match the movements of the persons they are facing, as though those persons were seeing themselves in a mirror. After a few minutes, tell the leaders and their mirror images to switch roles.

Arm-y of Love Game

You may want to play this game while some children are waiting to be picked up.

Say: David's army was ready to fight Saul, but David told them to love Saul instead. So, David had an army of love for Saul. Let's make an arm-y of love.

Have all of the children except one stand, arms linked, back-to-back, in a circle, facing outward. The one child left is to be passed around the circle by the children with linked arms. Arms should stay linked as the child is passed. Hugs along the way are encouraged. Enjoy the giggles and sillies from this game!

Sneaking Up on Saul

The children might wonder how David was able to sneak up on King Saul so that the king was not even aware of it. Use this game as an illustration for the story. Choose one child to be King Saul. The king will lie down on the floor and close his/her eyes, pretending to be asleep. Drape a small towel over the person who is King Saul. The object of the game is for the children, one at a time, to attempt to take the cloth without waking King Saul. If the king wakes up and says "Gotcha," the child who is holding the towel becomes the next King Saul. If no one has the towel when the King shouts "Gotcha," then the king goes back to sleep and another child makes the attempt.

Cops and Robbers

Use this game when you are talking about honesty. Hold up a bag of pennies. Select one child to be the Cop and stand in the center of the circle. Have the rest of the children stand in a circle shoulder to shoulder, facing the cop, with their hands held behind their backs. Go around the outside of the circle and place a penny or nothing in each child's hands. You must touch each child's hand to continue the deception. Caution the children that as soon as their hands are touched, they must close their fingers so that no one will know what they have, if they have anything. The object of the game is to deceive the policeman.When you have been all the way around the circle, tell the policeman that you have lost all your money. Someone has stolen it. The policeman must help you find it. The policeman can walk around the circle, looking intently at each person. If the policeman thinks that one of the children is hiding a coin, he or she says: "I think he's guilty!" The child who is accused must hold his or her hands out in front to prove the policeman right or wrong. If the thief is caught, then he or she must go to the center or "jail."

With Older Elementary

Bible Verse Balloon Toss:
Inflate eight balloons. With a soft permanent marker, write one word on each balloon from a Bible verse. Play music. Ask the students to keep the balloons in the air by hitting them up toward the ceiling. When the music stops, they should quickly grab the balloons and hold them in order so that the class can read the verse together. If you have eight students, each student should grab one balloon. If you have fewer students, let some of them hold two balloons. If you have a large class, you might want to make two sets of words, or divide the words into syllables. Repeat this activity as long as the children have interest. Then ask them to sit down and repeat the Bible verse as a group. Congratulate the class on memorizing the scripture for today.

Touching Others With a Smile
This game can be used in connection with the study of one of the Jewish Festivals: Rosh Hashannah and Yom Kippur. During this time the people tried new fruits to show that they were open to trying new things in life. This is also a solemn time of worship.
Have the children stand in a circle. (You may have to break them into smaller groups if you have a large class.)

Have each of the children choose a different fruit to be called. The object of the game is to see if the boys and girls can play it without smiling. Everyone must remain very solemn, because this is a solemn occasion. The boys and girls will call on each other trying to make them smile without smiling themselves.For example "kiwi kiwi calling banana banana." The person named banana would then pick another fruit and say "banana banana calling orange orange."

Let the children play the game. See how many children can keep from smiling. They all may break out in laughter. Assure them that even though we may have solemn occasions, God wants us to make everyone around us feel better and to keep smiling.

Truth or Lie
Play music as a signal for the students to gather in a circle. Tell the class that you are going to play a game called "Three Truths and a Lie". Begin the game by stating four things about yourself, three of which are true, and one which is a lie. (I am a Sunday school teacher, I own a

watch, I love my dog, I saw a snake in my garage this morning.) You will want to make the lie so subtle that the players will have to think. Other players guess which statement is a lie, then players take turns telling Three Truths and a Lie while others guess.

At the end of the game, be sure to discuss that sometimes people can get away with a lie; they will be totally believed. But God always knows! When a person is caught in a lie, they may not always be believed after that, even when they are telling the truth.

Fruits of the Spirit

Gather the children around a chalkboard or a large piece of paper. Tell the children you are going to play a game of "Build the Church". Draw three blanks on the chalkboard or paper. The object of this game is to identify the Fruits of the Spirit. The children will take turns guessing a letter that is in the name of the fruit, or guessing what the whole word is. Every time the children identify one of the Fruits of the Spirit, they will get to add another piece of the church. In order to build the entire church, we will have to guess all of the nine fruits. Have the children take turns guessing. If they guess a letter, and it is in the word, write that letter in the corresponding blank. It should not take them long to discover that the first fruit is "Joy". When they guess it, draw a horizontal line on the board (forming the floor of the church). Then, put up four blanks and have them guess "love". When they get it correct, draw a vertical line, forming one of the walls. Keep having them guess words by placing blanks for each letter of the Fruits of the Spirit. When they guess the third fruit, draw the second wall. The fourth gives them the ceiling, the fifth and sixth give them the roof, and the seventh and eighth give them the cross. Finally, have them guess the ninth to place the "rose window" in their church. (A rose window is a circular stained glass window common in many European churches.)

Planning the Worship

John 3:16

For God so loved
the world
that he gave his only
Son,
so that everyone
who believes in him
may not perish
but may have
eternal life.

(For) God

Make a "G" with the right hand, palm facing left, and point forward and up at the head level. Then move the right hand down and back toward the body, ending with an open palm facing left at chest level.

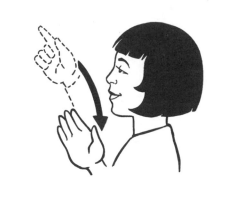

(so) loved

Cross both hands at the wrists and press them over the heart.

(the) world

Bring the right "W" hand, palm facing left and fingers pointed up, in a circle over and around the left "W" hand, palm facing right and fingers pointed out.

(that) he (God) gave

Hold both hands in front of the body, palms up and fingers and thumb touching on either hand. Then pull the hands in to the chest.

his (God) only

Extend the index finger of the right hand, palm facing out, and then twist the hand to the left so that the palm faces the body.

Son

Bring the thumb and extended fingers of the right hand to the right side of the forehead to grasp an imaginary cap brim. Then rock the arms together in the sign for "child."

(so that) everyone

Make fists with both hands, thumbs out. Hold up the left fist and with the thumb of the right fist, stroke down the left thumb. Then move the right hand out and up with the index finger extended.

who

Make a small counterclockwise circle with the right index finger in front of pursed lips.

believes (in him)

Touch the forehead with the right index finger. Bring the right hand down, palm flat, to meet the left hand, palm up, and clasp hands together.

(may) not

Place the right "A" hand under the chin. Move the thumb forward while moving the head from side to side, indicating "no."

perish

Hold the right palm up and the left palm down. Turn both hands over so that the right palm is down and the left palm is up.

but

Cross the index fingers of both hands in front of the body, then pull the hands apart.

(may) have

Touch the chest with the fingertips of both hands.

eternal

With the right hand held palm up, use the right index finger to trace a clockwise circle in the air. Then, with the right hand palm down in the "Y" position, move the hand straight forward.

life.

Form an "L" with both hands, palms facing the body and index fingers pointed toward each other. Move both "L" hands higher up in front of the body

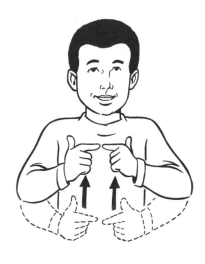

Sample Litanies

Faith

Leader: We come to you with open hearts, asking for your strength, O God.

All: Make our faith strong, Lord.

Leader: We come to you with joy in knowing that you are our God.

All: Make our faith full, Lord.

Leader: We come to you with doubts, with questions we cannot always answer.

All: Make our faith sure, Lord.

Leader: We come to you asking that you walk with us, beside us on our faith journey.

All: Guide us, Lord, along the way. Amen.

(From *Exploring Faith, Preteen Student, Summer 2002, Lesson 9,* Cay Barton)

O TASTE AND SEE THAT THE LORD IS GOOD

A Worship Litany

Christ the Lord is Risen Today.

Leader: Jesus, you surprise us with your presence.

Christ the Lord is Risen Today.

Leader: We are happy that you are alive!

Christ the Lord is Risen Today.

Leader: We are glad that you still lead us to God.

Christ the Lord is Risen Today.

Leader: We hear your voice in worship and song. We feel your presence in Communion.

Christ the Lord is Risen Today.

Leader: We know that you are God's Son and that because you live, we live also.

Christ the Lord is Risen Today.

Christ has died.
Christ is Risen.
Christ will come again.

(From *Exploring Faith, Preteen Student, Spring 2002, Lesson 5,* Ron Mills)

Psalm 23

Group 1: The Lord
Group 2: The Lord
Group 1: The Lord is my Shepherd.
Group 2: The Lord is our Shepherd.
Group 1: I shall have everything
Group 2: everything I need;
Group 1: You shall have everything,
Group 2: everything you need;
Group 1: we shall have everything.
Group 2: everything we need.

All: We shall have absolutely everything we need.

Response: The Lord's my Shepherd, I'll not want.

Group 1: The Lord makes me lie down
Group 2: in green pastures,
Group 1: leads me
Group 2: beside still waters;
Group 1: restores,
Group 2, refreshes,
Group 1 renews,
Group 2: replenishes,

Group 1: reinvigorates,
Group 2: revitalizes,
Group 1: repairs,
Group 2: resurrects,
All: restores my soul!

Group 1: The Lord leads me
Group 2: in right paths
Group 1: simply because
Group 2: that's who the Lord is.

All: and that's what the Lord does.

Response: The Lord's my Shepherd, I'll not want.

All: Even though I walk

Group 1: through the darkest valley;
Group 2: the deepest, darkest valley;
Group 1: I fear no evil,
Group 2: I fear no evil,

All: we fear no evil;

Group 1: for you, Lord,
Group 2: are with me.

O TASTE AND SEE THAT THE LORD IS GOOD

Group 1: Your rod
Group 2: and your staff

All: give me comfort.

Response: The Lord's my Shepherd, I'll not want.

ALL: In the presence of my enemies you prepare for me

Group 1: a snack,
Group 2: a light lunch,
Group 1: a full meal,
Group 2: a banquet,

All: a veritable feast!

Group 1: In the presence of my enemies
Group 2: you anoint my head with oil,
Group 1: you treat me like royalty,
Group 2: you bring me healing.
Group 1: In the presence of my enemies
Group 2: your blessing pours out upon me.

All: like an overflowing cup

Response: The Lord's my Shepherd, I'll not want.

Group 1: Surely goodness
Group 2: and mercy
Group 1: shall follow me,
Group 2: shall follow you,
All: shall follow us all the days of our life;

Group 1: and we shall dwell,
Group 2: in the house of the Lord
Group 1: forever,
Group 2: and ever,
Group 1: and ever,
Group 2: and ever,

All: our Shepherd forever and ever. Amen!

Response: The Lord's my Shepherd, I'll not want.

Psalm 23 adaptation by James Ritchie. The response line is the first line of hymn no. 36 in *The United Methodist Hymnal* and may be sung to that tune. (CRIMONDO)

The Image Declaration

I am male.

AND I AM CREATED IN THE IMAGE OF GOD.

I am female.

AND I AM CREATED IN THE IMAGE OF GOD.

I am tall.

AND I AM CREATED IN THE IMAGE OF GOD.

I am short.

AND I AM CREATED IN THE IMAGE OF GOD.

I am dark-skinned.

AND I AM CREATED IN THE IMAGE OF GOD.

I am light-skinned.

AND I AM CREATED IN THE IMAGE OF GOD.

I am able-bodied.

AND I AM CREATED IN THE IMAGE OF GOD.

I have special needs.

AND I AM CREATED IN THE IMAGE OF GOD.

**ALL: WE ARE ALL ALIKE.
WE ARE ALL DIFFERENT.
WE ALL BELONG TO GOD.**

(*Exploring Faith Preteen Student, Fall 2000, Leaflet 6,*
Ron Mills)

O TASTE AND SEE THAT THE LORD IS GOOD

A Beatitude Litany:

Leader: When Jesus saw the crowds, he went up the mountain; and after he sat down, his disciples came to him. Then he began to speak, and taught them, saying:

Group A: Blessed are the poor in spirit, for theirs is the kingdom of heaven.

Group B: Blessed are those who mourn, for they will be comforted.

Group C: Blessed are the meek, for they will inherit the earth.

Group A: Blessed are those who hunger and thirst for righteousness, for they will be filled.

Group B: Blessed are the merciful, for they will receive mercy.

Group C: Blessed are the pure in heart, for they will see God.

Group A: Blessed are the peacemakers, for they will be called children of God.

Group B: Blessed are those who are persecuted for righteousness sake for theirs is the kingdom of heaven.

Group C: Blessed are you when people revile you and persecute you and utter all kinds of evil against you falsely on my account.

Leader: Rejoice and be glad, for your reward is great in heaven, for in the same way they persecuted the prophets who were before you.
Matthew 5:1-12 (NRSV)

Sample Prayers

God, just a prayer for the snow.
Beautiful! Nice work! And a day off
from classes! Nice combination!
Protect those who have to drive in all
this. May they also see how beautiful
it is even as they have to come and
go in it. Thanks for the fun I intend to
have real soon! God bless everyone
in the snow! Amen!

From *Hey God, Let's Talk!* © 2000 Abingdon Press

I hear, O God, that
You need us to tell others!
You need us to talk about our faith!
You need us to show your love,
to make
Jesus known in us!
I pray I will be part of those who
will be not only hearers of your Word,
but doers of the Word as well.
As Isaiah
instructed us:
"My witnesses are you," says the Lord God.
"My servant whom I have chosen,
to the end that you may take thought
and believe in me."
Isaiah 43:10 (paraphrased)

From *Hey God, Let's Talk!* © 2000 Abingdon Press

O TASTE AND SEE THAT THE LORD IS GOOD

God,

The Bible says to be thankful at all times. This is hard to do, especially when I think that a situation is unfair. When I get angry, all kinds of negative thoughts come rushing into my mind.

But maybe that's the point of being thankful. If I could debate with myself, I'd ask, "What is good about what happened?"

I'll try to think positively, and maybe I'll find a solution, an alternative, or a new perspective. Amen.

On the mountain,
in the valley, by the sea
on the shore;
on the dance floor,
near the football field,
on the court;
in the church, in the classroom,
and while asleep;
watching TV, "kicking back,"
holding hands,
and slapping backs;
in quiet and with
stereo booming, in sickness,
and in health,
whether sad or glad,
your name be praised!
Amen!

A Vision of Hope

We pray that someday an arrow will be broken, not in something or someone, but by each of humankind, to indicate peace, not violence.

Someday, oneness with creation, rather than domination over creation, will be the goal to be respected.

Someday fearlessness to love and make a difference, will be experienced by all people.

Then the eagle* will carry our prayer for peace and love, and the people of the red, white, yellow, brown, and black communities can sit in the same circle together to communicate in love and experience the presence of the Great Mystery in their midst.

Someday can be today for you and me. Amen.

*An eagle in the Native American tradition is often a carrier of prayer.

Attributed to Wanda Lawrence, Chippewa, 20th Century from *The Untied Methodist Book of Worship,* © 1992, The United Methodist Publishing House.

Dear God, it's Monday again. I'm still sleepy from staying up late. I don't have all my homework done, and it looks like I will not get it finished. Help me through this day Lord, and help me to do better in the future. Amen.

From *Hey God, Let's Talk!* © 2000 Abingdon Press

O TASTE AND SEE THAT THE LORD IS GOOD

God, give us the wisdom to make good choices. Help us to realize temptation's scheme. When we fail, bring us back. Let us use our freedom to choose the life you would have us live. Amen.

(From *Exploring Faith, Preteen Student, Fall 2000, Leaflet 8,* Ron Mills.)

A Prayer of Confession

O Lord, our God
We confess that we often do not do what
    we know we ought to do.
We ignore those who need us the most.
We mislead others when it suits our
    purposes.
We think about ourselves first and others
    later.
We fail to be as faithful to you as we
    should be.
Forgive us, we pray.
Help us to lead lives more pleasing to
    you.
Guide us in the right direction, that our
    lives may be a blessing,
Both for ourselves and for others. Amen.

From *Exploring Faith, Preteen, Student Magazine, Fall 2001, Leaflet 11,* James Wrede

O God of great silence
who speaks a Word,
I will be silent now
(for as long as it takes)
before I begin my prayers
of praise or confession
or thanks or requests.
Praying needs some
peace and quiet don't you think?
Amen.

From *Hey God, Let's Talk!* © 2000 Abingdon Press

Directions for Liturgical Dance

Play "Spirit of the Living God" from the CD. It can also be found on page 393 in *The United Methodist Hymnal*. Have each team member close his or her eyes as the music plays to get the feel of the music.

Then select a leader. The leader will demonstrate each of the moves for the song. Then the group members will repeat the moves. Continue until everyone in the group feels comfortable with the movements. Then as a group plan how you will present the liturgical dance to the rest of the group during worship.

Spirit of the living God,
(Reach hands skyward, palms up.)

fall afresh on me.
(With bowed heads, bring hands down to the side, palms turned toward the body but not touching it.)

(Repeat)

Melt me
(Draw hands and head into the body, hold legs together, bend knees, move body slowly toward the floor.)

Mold Me
(Wrap arms around the body and slowly stand up, turning the body slightly from side to side at the same time.)

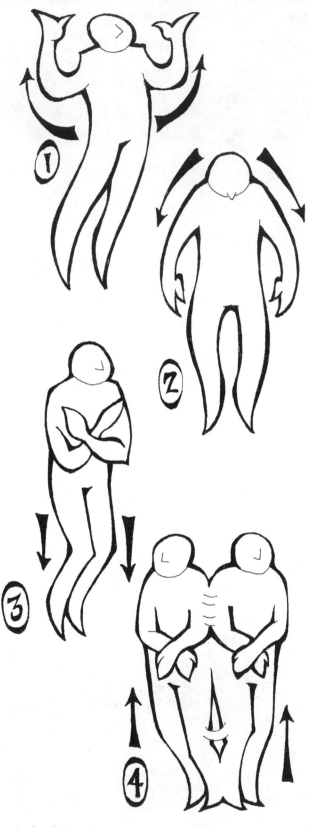

O TASTE AND SEE THAT THE LORD IS GOOD

Fill me
(Let the arms hang by your side. Bring your hands together, palms up below the waist, then move your arms and hands up to the top of your head.)

Use me
(Palms move to a side-by-side position as the hands and the arms begin to move out in front of the body, hands separate as the arms move down level with the waist.)

Spirit of the living God,
(Repeat the first movement)

fall afresh on me.
(Repeat the second movement.)

Adapted from *Exploring Faith: Older Elementary, Summer 2002,* © 2002 by Cokesbury.

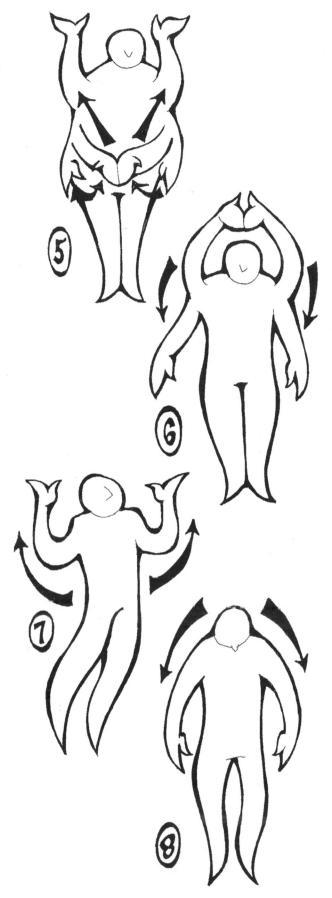

Names for Jesus:

Every one of the following Bible verses gives us a name (or two) for Jesus. Do you know what they are?

Acts 2:36
Luke 19:10
John 1:51
Matthew 12:8
Matthew 20:31
Revelation 22:16
Romans 12:5
John 21:7
Matthew 8:25
Acts 16:15
Revelation 1:8
John 1:1
John 6:48
John 8:12

O TASTE AND SEE THAT THE LORD IS GOOD

Bibliography

Brain Research Resources

General Overview
Carter, R. *Mapping the Mind*
Howard, P. *The Owner's Manual for the Brain*
Robertson, I. *Mind Sculpture: Unlocking Your Brain's Untapped Potential*

Teaching and Learning
Armstrong, T. *Awakening Genius in the Classroom*
Dennison & Dennison, *The Brain Gym*
Gelb, M. *How to Think Like Leonardo da Vinci Workbook*

Jensen, E. *Teaching With the Brain in Mind*
Oliver, C. & Bowler, R. *Learning to Learn*
Ornstein, T.R. *The Amazing Brain*
Sunbeck, D. *Infinity Walk: Preparing Your Mind to Learn*
Sylvester, R. *A Biological Brain in a Cultural Classroom*
Sylvester, R. *Celebration of Neurons: An Educator's Guide to the Human Brain*
Goleman, D. *Emotional Intelligence*

Teaching Resources

Bruce, B. *Our Spiritual Brain*
Bruce, B. *7 Ways of Teaching the Bible to Children*
Flegal, D. *More Sign and Say: Bible Verses for Children*
Flegal, D. *Play & Say: Bible Verses for Children*
Flegal, D. *Sign and Say: Bible Verses for Children*
Flegal, D. *Sing & Say: Bible Verses for Children*
Flegal, D., Stickler, L., & St. John, J. *Don't Get Wet Feet and 50 Other Bible Stories for Preschoolers*
Flegal, D., Stickler, L., & St. John, J. *The Jailhouse Rocked and 50 Other Bible Stories for Elementary Children*
Flegal, D., Stickler, L., & St. John, J. *Ring 'Round Jericho and 50 Other Bible Games for Preschoolers*
Flegal, D., Stickler, L., & St. John, J. *Downright Upright and 50 Other Bible Games for Elementary Children*
Flegal, D., Stickler, L., & St. John, J. *Footprints on the Wall and 50 Other Bible Crafts for Preschoolers*
Flegal, D., Stickler, L., & St. John, J. *From Bags to Bushes and 50 Other Bible Crafts for Elementary Children.*
Flegal, D., Stickler, L., & St. John, J. *Holy Moses Stomp and Other Music Activities for Preschoolers*
Flegal, D., Stickler, L., & St. John, J. *Rockin' Rainsticks and Other Music Activities for Elementary Children*
Halverson, D. *The Nuts & Bolts of Christian Education: Practical Wisdom for Teachers & Leaders*
Halverson, D. *32 Ways to Become a Great Sunday School Teacher*
Miller, L.R. & Flegal, D. *Holy Moses Stomp and Other Music Activities for Preschoolers*
Miller, L.R. & Flegal, D. *Rockin' Rainsticks and Other Music Activities for Elementary Children*
Roehlkepartain, J. *Teaching Kids to Care & Share*
Stoner, *Teaching Tips for Terrified Teachers*
Stickler, L. *Out of the Box*
Younger, B & Flinn, L. *Flood Punch, Bowl Bread, and Group Soup*
Stoner, M. *Signs of the Faith*
Terrell, C. *Hey, God, Let's Talk! Teaching Children About Prayer*

Books to Share With Children
For Preschoolers

Curtis, J. L. *Today I Feel Silly*
Brown, M.B. *The Runaway Bunny*
Flegal, D. *Bible Says*
Flegal, D. *Jesus Says*
Flegal, D. *Paul Says*
Flegal, D. and Augustine, P. *Alphabet Rhymes for Bible Times*
Hudson, W. *God Smiles When*
Joosse, B. *Mama, Do You Love Me*

Lester, H. *Tacky the Penguin*
Parry, A. & L. *Badger's Lovely Day*
Parry, A. & L. *Goodnight Prayers*
Parry, A. & L. *Mouse Can't Sleep*
Parry, A. & L. *Never Mind Squirrel*
Parry, A. & L. *Rabbit Helps Out*
Penn, A. *The Kissing Hand*
Thomas, S.T. *Somewhere Today*

For Younger Elementary

Brumbeau, J. *The Quiltmaker's Gift*
Buckley, R. The Wing
Buckley, R. God's Love Is Like
Buckley, R. The Give-Away
Cowen-Fletcher, J. *It Takes a Village*
de Paola, T. *The Parables of Jesus*
de Paola, T. *Book of Bible Stories*
Hearth, A.H. Reach High
Jeffs, S. *If You'd Been There in Bible Times*
Kushner L. & K. *Because Nothing Looks Like God*

Ladwig, T. *The Lord's Prayer*
Ladwig, T. *Psalm Twenty-three*
Pennington, T. *Fishing with Granddaddy B.*
Sasso, S.E. *God In Between*
Sasso, S. *In God's Name*
Spier, P. *Noah's Ark*
Spier, P. T*he Book of Jonah*

O TASTE AND SEE THAT THE LORD IS GOOD